HΛVİN9 NONE OF İT

Also by
Adrienne Su

Middle Kingdom

Sanctuary

HAVING NONE OF IT

adrienne su

manic d press
san francisco

Published by Manic D Press. For information, contact Manic D Press,
PO Box 410804, San Francisco CA 94141   www.manicdpress.com

Cover photograph © Regina Catharina Fernandi Paassen
Printed in the USA

Library of Congress Cataloging-in-Publication Data

Su, Adrienne, 1967-
  Having none of it / Adrienne Su.
    p. cm.
  ISBN 978-1-933149-27-1 (trade pbk.)
  1. Chinese Americans--Poetry. I. Title.
  PS3569.U13H38 2009
  811'.54--dc22
                                    2008050002

contents

For my Brother
jonaThan su

I

THE Pen

must have heft,
its job being physical;

can't afford to apologize
with a ladylike barrel;

must, because its owner
is not, be dependable;

and, serving perchance
as the solitary vehicle

of frank deliberation,
or as central receptacle

of quotidian detail for its
seemingly nonverbal

companion in exile,
ought to be refillable

with insomnia, regret,
elation, impossible

plans, and the tedious
ache of perennial

relinquishment, the only way
out of which is the ritual

of lifting the instrument
with intent to unravel

the thread of ink that turns
into flesh as it travels.

on NOT writing in cafés
for S. W.

It's too much like sex in a car:
fine as a concept (everyone needs
to be seen at times by strangers),
but reality seldom agrees.

It's clumsy. Whoever happens
along as you start to forget yourself
is not what you fancied – a relation,
a stranger you know too well.

The hand that isn't holding the pen
flails like an animal pinned by a leg.
And the gorgeous epiphany, just then
at the tip of your tongue, has fled.

Love

Not being in it or even in one of its empty forms,
I can see it for what it is: minor-to-major illness,
interferer with plans, abandoner of friends,
root cause of insomnia and death of appetite,
inconvenience making its holder ridiculous.

I say "holder" even though it sounds ridiculous
because I dislike the word "lover" for suggesting the illicit
and/or continuous action, as clearly one can love
while doing other things – as most of the time,
even when unable to think of anything but the beloved,

that's what people do – but to love and be loved
is apparently not the same as to inhale and exhale,
or to have a circulatory system, or to be,
with or without affection. Such prejudicial usage
is nearly as unfair as this cold spring day

on which the shoots of irises have risen halfway,
catalogs overflow with swimsuits that swear
to correct all lacks and excesses, and there's ice
on the patio, where I'd be reading if it were warmer
and if nature didn't always interfere, raining

bugs or blowing the pages or just plain raining
on the *Week in Review* the moment I begin
to comprehend the destruction we've wrought
in – where was it? – another distant land from which
sons and daughters keep coming back ruined.

THE COUNTDOWN

We'd unleashed the dogs of war,
not even sure what the bone of contention,
said to be buried in the backyard, was anymore.

No treaty had a dog's chance, or a Chinaman's,
against what crashed to the ground
when the clouds opened. We would've been

fine with cats & dogs. But no one was there
to make the lion lie down; the bull
had toured the china shop, and shards

lay all over the bed. So there we were
when night fell, bone-tired, with nowhere
to sleep but the freshly cleared earth,

which we didn't even circle three times.

POST

We've not only ousted the dictator,
we've also finished reveling in it:
ripped down portraits, hauled off furniture,
danced in the alleys, let the artists

out of jail. Everyone's feeling heady
still, despite the agenda: rehabilitate
teachers, fix roads and factories,
reunite families, sort the mass graves,

catalogue evidence. It isn't a party.
Some things will smell; there may be violence.
And – patience – the limping economy
can't sustain reparations. The extravagance

of founding day has passed. We know
people crave another hour of resurrection,
long-forbidden light on long-closed
eyes, the embrace of the mother or son

despaired of, the clean vindications,
freedom to talk. Everyone cherished
the waving from tanks, the radiant reception
of peacekeepers as they established

their posts. We all want to feel like that
again, and will in time, but no future
worth receiving will descend as fast
as a tyrant's head. We're nearly a desert

island now, without schools or a roof;
we're a broken aqueduct trying to reach
a metropolis. An army without boots.
We're an ancient language nobody speaks;

our national anthem has gone unplayed
so long, our children can barely recite it.
We're the final book in a smoldering library,
waiting for literate eyes. May nothing ignite it.

THE grave

is inaccessible because the land, as ever,
is someone else's, or because the body never
existed, or wasn't acknowledged. The future

keeps barreling in like the clumsiest burglar,
hoping to be caught. Even I could capture
the fool, but then what? He's just another

symptom of trouble. And it's time to mourn
my buried love. Go on, break down the door,
I know what you want and it can't be forced

or threatened out. Rage or rant, the entity
that matters is going fast to flowers, its history
unmoored, and I've got to touch it again, if only

in memory's den or the garden of language,
even if parts are missing or damaged,
through being the only way out of the carnage.

inheritance

The house, seized; cash, devalued; animals,
given away; the rest, too heavy for travel.

What we have to give: a talent for sacrifice.
Pirates took everything once, so they can twice.

The aftermath won't be as you imagine.
Such losses are finite, like the mountain

behind us. Waking with what mind made,
hands and feet will start without complaint,

follow through like soldiers. Hardest to build
is sense of place, but once you've willed

away the past, you'll find the soil soft,
each room yielding to the youngest blood

of history. Necessity will eat the doubts.
Relish that, as choice invades the house.

Few will believe your version of any
tale, or ask to hear it, but you'll be ready

for most species of silence, being used
to misinterpretation — common truth

to which few tune in. We hope you never hear
the rap at the door that landed us all so far

from go, but lest you be among those chosen
for rending, we present to you this fortune.

MiDDLe OF NOWHere

It's lost the doubleness of nowhere
being enough of a somewhere

to have a middle, but now that
I've lived here so long, now that

my Pennsylvanian children
are old enough to make reference

to a *middle of nowhere*, it makes
its way into the house in strange

new fashion. They say it without
contempt, as any old idiom, without

foreknowledge of how I'll take it.
And whoever I am, I no longer take it

as I used to deliver it. I hear
the *middle*; I don't hear

the *nowhere*. Because they were
made here, it's somewhere;

because I found you here,
it's somewhere,

even though it has to be explained
to everyone I meet in that alien

place I used to call matter-of-factly
the city.

in spite of great difficulty

the early years were easier, without
the question of what they were,
other than aliens who took their tea hot.

They didn't plan to stay forever.
They saw the soil as someone else's
and lived apart from the simmering

conflict, which seemed to call for
contenders lighter and darker
than themselves. Their papers

expired, then were unexpectedly
replaced. Slowly they ceased
to grasp the idiom of the recently

arrived. Suddenly there were children
singing the alphabet, skating on ice,
conspiring with American friends

against the neighborhood bully.
All arms and legs and hungry mouths,
the kids were the funniest newly-

made things they could have imagined.
Where the eldest got that overdone
means of explaining, or the little one

the hair that wouldn't sit flat, no one
could confirm, yet they were clearly
their parents' children. One afternoon,

their mother recalled, she'd run her
swollen fingers over her swollen middle
and told the bump, *Bless whoever you are,*

then wolfed the double-decker Reuben
she'd never wanted a bite of before.
Sometimes at night the father listened

to the giant silence that was the Pacific
and knew it wouldn't be broken.
So what if his son would never inherit

the family business the Communists
had seized? The boy had no mind for it,
rather, an artsy streak, and might've killed it.

Uprising followed uprising. The papers
reported little, and they had to be careful
not to fill the gaps with conjecture,

which was usually worse and led to other
things they feared, like the children's
potential poverty or grief, all-out failure

to thrive or, God forbid, dying young.
Since they'd grown accustomed to not
being able to protect the other ones

they loved, they sometimes switched
between exertions: too little, then too much.
They did their best, given the erratic shifts

of mind, sparked by the unexpected
(the taste of almonds; artificial orange),
which could dash their sense of place and resurrect

the old despair, from back when they felt sure
they'd left a thousand ancestors behind
with nothing to eat, and wound up nowhere.

some grandmothers

As far as we could tell,
their narratives were fictional:
opera, cinema, novels.

They weren't the type
to cook all night
for gatherings; they liked

to stay in bed and work
the crossword. They weren't
fawning; they had earned

the right to be stationary.
We regarded their reality
as forced monotony,

day upon day of leisure
with men they'd never
had passions for,

the children dispersed.
They seemed to endure
their potential. Now in earth,

they seem less quiescent.
Of course their adolescent
ambitions were silenced,

but so were everyone's.
They had room to imagine.
They could point to reasons

for the state of things
and weren't lesser beings
by virtue of anything.

Now we know whom they pitied.
We'd moved to fabulous cities
alone, created identities,

begun to be taken
seriously, then fallen
in love with convention

or at least come to crave it,
though we didn't admit it
and they didn't say it.

They knew we wouldn't listen.
Who'd believe a foreign woman
who had never let her talent

bloom, who always seemed
to live in fiction, who claimed
that when she dreamed

she was a butterfly,
she was a butterfly?
She might as well fly.

THE LOVE BOAT

Every summer a different handful disappeared, their whereabouts
explained at someone's house or on Lake Lanier:
Oh, Jimmy's on the Love Boat – tossed off as if it were a tour

of Europe or tennis camp or a cold. The following season
Jimmy would appear with a beautiful Chinese American who,
if she'd been one of us, would be out of his league;

she lived in Cincinnati and was writing him letters.
Later Jimmy or whoever it was would go north to college,
be a success, marry someone sweet – whether

of Chinese descent it didn't matter – and vanish in suburbia,
his teenage travels so remote, no one thought of them
for decades, until the core group convened in Atlanta

for yet another funeral and someone remarked *My children
refuse to learn Chinese.* Then someone else recalled
the tropical summers, the t'ai chi and calligraphy lessons,

the notion that it might be like the show with an Asian cast,
and all those cousinlike strangers whose parents hoped
to match them up with someone good enough to save the past

that seemed a little deader every time a daughter
brought home another white guy who loved her like crazy.
Once the best hope of the grandparents (remembered

from the margins of parties, hard to talk to, filling spring rolls
with a fluency that made them foreign), now it's an in-joke so far in
it's barely a joke: seldom told and funny only on days of sorrow.

THe women anD THe girls

Like punctuation, it had always been present,
just unnoticed. Nature had installed it, like her eggs:

a fundamental capacity to refuse,
kicking in as the young began to move

by independent effort. Where was she
who took out everyone's trash, gave up her sleep,

took belittlement to heart (though weeping),
paid any check, accepted raw everything,

and cooked it? Where the loving absorption,
hunched posture, the crazy proportion

of apology to fairness? It was as if
she'd been secretly murdered and some bitch

understudy thrust on stage, ready to eat
alive whoever dared drain away what

she'd struggled so many years to get
(a decade of waiting tables, sweatshop

cutwork, or cleaning strangers' homes,
it must have been, she was that damn

mad and done with false cheer). You couldn't
fight the thing; it had its own government,

like a natural disaster, and any who tried
would be washed away as if by flood

or avalanche, sputtering pointless words.
Most shocking of all was how standard

it had become; wherever you looked, others
had pitched that flag. It felt like junior

high, when one by one the girls began
to bleed, and what seemed at first a legion

of limits – embarrassing stuff to schlep
to school, breakouts, cramps, not standing up

for fear of stains – eventually had them remade.
It had to gestate, but once they'd chucked the shame,

no one could detect again that demure
inaction, those question marks of what they were.

WHY IT HAPPENED

When the question got out,
somebody answered it.

The troll in the meadow,
beast in the wood, wanted it

to be requited. You didn't believe
in the supernatural,

but there you were, in its province,
fluent as if by miracle.

Never expecting to be rewarded,
you were only feeding a hunger

nature had set you up to sate.
Your body took over, conquered

principle like land. You'd never
been chronically anything – late,

impulsive, hard to reach, or prey
to the easiest overtures – but today,

ambushed, you've let your mouth
get out of control. Out of your head

the word became. And such
was it done: because it was said.

DOUBLE HAPPINESS

One happiness
plus one happiness
make bliss.

Ideal: to be identical
in meaning and radical,
eternally parallel.

Each half androgynous
as a numeral, differences
of animus

erased by calligraphy,
the word is a warranty
against everyday acrimony,

rage and refusal.
If one of the couple
becomes a brick wall

or a rope or a hammer,
both must remember
the nuptial erasure

on which the kingdom's
dominion depends.
It was never for them.

Breakup

Another ending finds its place
among novels, lives, summers
that fled, but this kind has a way
of getting filed under failure:

yes, the relationship failed,
if to fail is to fail to endure.
Although it's already
impossible to remember

what made it work, if it did,
certain things stick: the glint
of sun off your car at the side
of a country road, the exit

I took to reach your house,
your miraculous ability
not to mythologize, and the doubt.
Now that it's all turned instantly

into a shut book, it's been stained
the shade of its defeat, like the life
of a suicide. I can't understand
how I entered it, can't revive

the radiance my mind insists
surrounded us once. Now it says
I knew all along but distrusted it.
Why should I trust it now? It says

we won't meet again, and this time
it's quoting you. So here's my goodbye
to you, your house, and the sunlight
of contentment. You're a diary

chapter now, happy right up
to the end, when what I knew
became what I felt. That is not what
failure is. That is me and you.

in THE waKe

Gatherings split, by accident
or law, into genders. The blouse
that used to be funky takes on

troubling connotations; innocent
lipsticks harbor hot-pink agendas;
even business reeks of infringement.

Other moms with their superclean
children seem to tuck them
into skirt lengths, despite jeans;

in daylight your hands look naked,
almost obscene. At the ladies'-room sink
the phantom ring seems fated

to be washed away. At meetings
you automatically cover your fingers
as if they were legs, but by evening

they're almost perfect. Later a stranger
will declare them sacred, press them
to his palms. It'll be night, you'll linger

in the pearly light of redemption,
there'll be dinner, you'll marvel at
how close you came to obliteration

and just as in the weeks postpartum
forget the violence
that delivered the gift. It isn't

going to look like bliss, but in its service
you'll have to learn not to ask
anymore, *What did I do to deserve this?*

THe Amazing ParT

is how terrible it isn't, how flat,
how tidily calm, as what I wanted
turns out to be what I wanted.

Not ruinous or cruel, not wrapped
in vengefulness, it sleeps beside me,
warm as a husband or baby.

It holds the future like flowers,
opens doors, helps as I navigate
puddles. It even shares my taste

in books, doesn't find them obscure.
At moments it seems to resemble
the past, but that's because the available

forms are few. And I'm scrupulous,
aware it'll one day surrender
to a thing so familiar, all will appear

to have been for no purpose.
I accept. It's the nature of nature.
Even regrets undergird this composure,

itself a kind of marriage, if not passion.
Therefore I take with equanimity
if not quite festivity

the hand of this anti-lover in absence,
on whom my presence depends.
I'll not step into that river again.

Doglessness

As with other chronic conditions,
I'd grown used to it and couldn't
feel the chill. It seemed an economy:
acres of time, money, energy

freed, appointments canceled
daily. Indoors, I imagined myself
imagining. At the gym, despite
all evidence, I thought I might

arrive one day, as if movement
could be spent on oneself without
cost. Morning to night, I went with
others of my species and didn't wish

for everything we'd done again
and again and again back when,
nor for the day I'd re-enter
the wordless contract, sure

to end in grief. I could just about
see how those, content without,
made sense. Domestic perfection,
pick-up-and-go. Such repetition—

I could've been brilliant or rich.
(I even baked for the bitch.)
But isn't that how it is when love
goes underground? Of a sudden,

weekends, seasons, decades
rewrite themselves as waste.
You can't recall the falling in. If
you do, it's into a fiery pit.

The stupid self who put you here
must've been blind from youth or
a gaze. She didn't know the future
from which you critique her,

and the question isn't whether
but which. Despise or forgive her:
she'll go back, and if anyone's going to
understand why or how, it's you.

ODE TO A LIPSTICK

Clinique's "All Heart"

Unable to separate shade from name,
I wear it as reminder.

Close to my nature, not earth, not flame,
It forces the behavior

Of one who speaks and acts in harmony
With her inner style

Because her lips are the color of honesty
And a little guile.

T. J. Maxx
for N. K.

It's all about what could've happened.
On every tag, the shaded portion

marked COMPARE AT asserts
the fortune being saved, never

mind that you wouldn't have bought it.
It's as good as cash in hand, credit

toward education, airfare to Xanadu.
We separate at first, then rendezvous

at the fitting room, our alternate
lives on hangers, and walk in and out

of dimensions. Regarding each other
as starlets, jocks, ambassadors,

we laugh so hard we barely need
to buy, and nourish the fantasy

that we're who the clothes
were made for, though most

need hemming or pleating.
You at a garden party, meeting

the one you shouldn't have left.
Me and the one I should've...

Of course it isn't practical.
We don't come here to be sensible.

When we have a sense of time again
and stagger with our bargains

into the boiling lot, the sun so sharp
we can't tell where we parked,

we prepare to make the journey
back to the foreign country

where the money we would have wasted
if we'd shopped at other places

is irrelevant
because we didn't.

II

Having it All

We bought the concept like a dress
we'd never wear to anything;
it simply looked too fabulous.

Now that the emperor's shivering
in his skin, our lives are half done,
the family hungry and clamoring

for its share of what we promised
to lavish, back when we were flush.
Not that we don't want to give it—

we can feel it in our breasts,
the generosity we've become,
but at times it is our very flesh

that resists when we offer it up.
There won't be anything left,
it would say if it could, *and what*

will become of the little ones then?
Once we were a bottomless well.
Once we were mighty as men;

we talked and drank and loved
as fiercely—oh, how they loved us back!
Then one day love or whatever it was

ceased to be just for the fun of it.
The event that completed us undid
the cloth. And now we'll have none of it.

Fricassee au Poulet

When she caught herself trying
not to eat it, not because

she didn't like it or wasn't hungry
or thought she was fat, but because,

lacking strength to cook again,
she wanted it to last two nights,

she understood whose flesh lay
prostrate on the bed of Pyrex,

torn by those she cherished.
A conclusion with no apparent

beginning, it had simply arrived
like a brush fire, like a boot on an ant,

and nurture levels hit a new low.
Just like that. She rewound a little:

garlic, onions, rosemary, wine,
a chicken, olives and their oil,

a process she used to savor.
Now it almost hurt. How a passion

could travel the world, then fall
into such an obvious trap, she hadn't

the faintest, but now her bones
were up for grabs. She'd be reviled

by some for what was going to happen,
but the choice was false: their approval

or her kids. That blinding minute
she would have made the leap for sure

if it hadn't been made ahead for her
like a frozen dinner – just heat & serve.

March comes in like a Lion

Just as it was growing possible to love what others love
The numbness that opens with the narcissus
The dream-deflating lightness of bedcovers
Insidious granting of wishes

No excuse to lament by the window the truth of each matter
The melt having unburied the dead again
As blossoms vie for attention in the obvious manner
The voice upon the snowy hush unable to be heard again

1989

Stamped on our diplomas, it lived in neither future
nor past, only the eternity in which we sweated:
the summer between education and whatever
it had prepared us for, the rooms we'd rented,

their humidity, and mutual advice on not-quite
boyfriends we didn't hope to wed but whose interim
deals made us mad. Seize the day, we'd been taught.
The day was too hot. Nights, we talked above the hum

of fans, from lumpy beds, across an absence of hall,
about what we knew we did not. *This is what it means,*
one of us would announce. The mini-fridge stalled,
curdled the milk. We asked the sun not to rise, took turns

turning twenty-two – and summer had run. The lease
expired; both of us moved; then most of the nation
lay between us. We called and wrote. The first divorce
seemed to drop from a cloud. Rain and attrition

turned letters to cards. Seventeen summers later
I was painting the door, meaning to repair my life
with a brush. *You're too old for this,* I said to whoever
I'd become. At the ringing of the phone, it was otherwise

still an ordinary day.
                         Now you're a portrait, a song
in my head, and we're talking again on how to live.
I know it isn't fair to say *we.* But *I* would be wrong,
your absence being the presence that, taken, gives.

knowledge

The nearest thing to religion
we had – the more the better –
it seemed an improbable sin.

More prescription than temptation,
it was the heart of the dream
and might have been Confucian.

Keenly aware of how else it could be,
neither parent pushed us
to be millionaires or prodigies,

but pressed instead a higher
sense of sanctity. It was always
better to know and consider

than pretend the offending
idea had vanished.
Of course there were things

you didn't say to children,
but sometime in their teens
the world of folly and wisdom

would be theirs to investigate.
Sure, there were nations
quick to incarcerate

whoever asked the wrong questions,
but they were backward
totalitarian lands. If an American

had ever been denounced
for being inquisitive,
it had ended on the playground

where the bully who made a habit
of beating up smart boys would growl
It's a free country before letting them have it.

Even the overachievers had Barbies

Since she'd already been beheaded,
we didn't concern ourselves much
with her looks. We focused instead
on her stuff, the shoes and sumptuous

dresses, cars that never broke down,
the townhouse done up in pink. Although
she seemed to have no job or husband,
she'd apparently paid it all off, with no

ill effects on sleep or complexion.
Her age was ambiguous: fully adult
but younger than every woman
we knew. Although we never bought

a Ken, we knew they had a marital life
when we weren't looking. We blocked out
the details, but she'd picked him for all the right
reasons: he was clever and funny, a knockout

in bed, good-looking, an acceptable color.
We didn't consider the health effects
of her chosen form of birth control or
the obvious boob job; we didn't expect

to wake up one morning to hear another
fight about the Visa bill or who would
take off work to wait for the plumber.
We never heard the silence that followed

or the quarterly talks about how children
would ruin their lifestyle, or how
she fended off her therapist's attempts
to help her re-imagine her life without

the uncertainty. We always got better
grades than she, but continued taking refuge
in her tiny living room, rose-colored shelter
from what our intelligence couldn't refuse.

Reading

You know yourself. Any form of it
can be a source of nourishment
if you're sensitive to the instinct
and reveries that point out the text

each circumstance demands. This
comes easily to those who've taken
their years with reckless caution,
stopping just short of the precipice

often enough to apprehend existence
as cartoonish, yet irreversible.
Having been seduced by powerful
authors whose memory makes you wince

today, you know in the end you'll fail
to build the perfect temple, but keep
on digging. Every twelve years you read
Anna Karenina again, just in case,

but otherwise there's no particular
plan, just a well-developed sense
of bibliography. Whatever happens
to be selling well, you're already sure,

from practice in feeling and thought,
of your chosen adventure, however
obscure or out-of-print. Advertisers
hate people like you, who ought

to be excellent customers but who,
thanks to a certain attitude
toward your history (the usual
series of errors, crimes, doomed

beginnings, minor victories),
could walk into the largest
bookstore in the universe
and sniff out the very story,

poem, or novel, from among
the whole bewildering range,
that was sent by a stranger
who quietly fashioned it in some

overpopulated shack polluted
by television, specifically
for you, whoever you might be,
to receive in grateful solitude.

Men Alone

No more do we mock their wrinkled shirts,
the clumped spaghetti they offered
with mortification, requiring comfort.

Even in college, sprawled across their beds
to talk of aspirations or the sexes,
we knew we'd sailed into the heart of fairness.

It lacked suspense but brimmed with advantages:
double the friends, equality, access,
someone to offer the other perspective.

Give came with take, for time was abundant.
Girlfriends still made the best girlfriends,
wives did too much of the work of husbands,

but now we were equal: now *we* could drop
our clothes wherever we shed them, and none
would be wasted in bitterness, picking them up.

Housekeeping

Properly done, it seldom calls for words.
Even as it taxes the arms, it asserts

an inner order, by joint exertion
of established means and innovation.

Daily it yields the impeccable floor
the mind, to be emptied, requires,

as mind inhabits body, which asks
for shelter, the cleaning of which exacts

more than we wish to pay. We'd all prefer
the leisure to work on chapter or verse,

and not to bake them into gingerbread.
But many a muse has gently demurred

when asked to enter a squalid kitchen;
they are, in spite of everything, old women,

trained to discern domestic barrenness,
to cut down every obstacle to cleanliness.

So use them. Ask them if you're apt to be
remembered for your lemon cake and tea

and the way you governed goings-on
in your earthly domicile, or for your songs.

THE SLIGHTEST SIGN

What if it turned out to be a truant,
a corporate thug or embezzler,
a landlord who stole from tenants?
Would she retrace the steps of her
diary, tasting every glass of wine
she'd had before they knew, measure
the stress of her job, count the times
she dreamed she'd given birth

to a beast? So often she'd woken up
relieved that thoughts couldn't cross
the placenta, then wondered what
made her so sure, she tried to erase
from her psyche all kinds of misery:
forgetting to take her lunch to school,
insomnia, attempted rape, the history
of women who'd broken the rules.

Unlike the ancients, she would never
have to drown herself in apology—
would she? At times she didn't feel sure.
But when she felt the future contentedly
turning inside her, minuscule, imperative,
cute as hell and already pushing her limits,
she decided – as if there were alternatives –
to embrace it, and all that came with it.

in labor

Those who've been there understand
the choice of preposition: not *at* or *on*,
not *through* or *under*. Labor's a stanza,

room into which no one follows entirely.
A good midwife gets to the doorjamb;
exceptional nurses hang behind her, calmly

assessing your voice. The father, however
sensitive or kind, turns instantly inept,
a gesturing fool locked out forever.

Looking back from the side of the cliff,
you wonder how you ever trusted this
mortal whose cheerful ovations are rife

with presumptuous ignorance. How
would *he* be able to tell if *you* were
doing great? Pain, like Charon, rows

you across into hell; as labor's language
translates into curses in your own,
you take all names in vain, then engage

with the only person here who's having
as tough a time as you, the one who wants
to exit the stanza. Labor's the hardest-working

working vacation, last unequivocal getaway
in a long line of days. Once upon a time
you could be bought with nifty sayings

like *mind over matter* or *love conquers
all* – but love turns out sometimes to be
helpless, and mind to be made out of matter.

goddess / sybil / lactation consultant

At the mom-and-baby support group, the lesson of the week:
If Mom isn't happy, nobody's happy.
She says it with the gravitas of a dozen PhDs,

she who weighed my newborn with a length of cloth, not the cold
    metal tray,
she who arranged us in bed so baby could eat and mom could sleep,
she who taught us to evade infection by sending the milk on its way.

Mothers murmur assent, some with knowing laughs.
Babies squirm. Then, suggestions from the floor:
Make a list of chores and make your husband do half;

don't stay in pajamas all day, no matter how much you're leaking;
don't be afraid to ask for help; keep crackers by the bed
so you won't have to choose between sleeping and eating.

Too busy to return for weeks, I kept the advice in what was left
of my brain. It began to work miracles: the more the baby ate,
the more the milk came down, as if a mother's breast

were the magic porridge pot of lore, saving the village,
never running low. But that's where the parallel
ends, unless your version of the tale's the one in which

the pot takes offense at insult or abuse, and resigns.
The gift of my goddess / sybil / lactation consultant
was the thousand tiny steps by which I climbed

the mountain of requisite happiness, at whose summit
I hit the border that would make me illegal,
an immigrant in the land of beatific

post-apocalypse, washing plates or bringing out Sternos
for a buffet the like of which my ancestors never saw.
My daughters would be its guests someday, even though

their mom had come in at the bottom, bedraggled
and heavy with milk, afraid of what she knew
she had to do, readying her papers for officials

and counting on the mostly absent little one
to keep the milk from turning against her,
and the little one counting on her, to map the region.

THE BABY YEARS

went unrecorded, eclipsed
by sleep in winks, the swiftest
showers, three-minute eggs.

Nothing before had escaped
examination. Then night and day
married and collapsed;

reflection came only in mirrors.
As if she'd meant at first to go
elsewhere, she seems in pictures

benignly surprised, a speaker
cut off mid-sentence and conquered
by accidental joy – as if an old

standby had broken and a better version
been repaired. One afternoon
the doubt disappears, the dogged

proving, the stream of questions…
Nestled in pillows, exhaustion,
laundry, books without words,

she comprehends the centuries
of silence, the vocabulary
never learned from flash cards

or study abroad. It's there
in cookbooks, in how her mother
makes a bed, in the melody

that stops the crying. And she'd nearly
missed it, so buried she'd been
in definitions. She can almost give in.

CHILD

Sometime in the second year, I saw it:
her consciousness, fully separate
from all I said and did for her,
from every event that was to come.
It was almost a spirit, except it was trapped
in a small, seemingly inexperienced body.

There were ways in which I could encourage it.
I could read out loud until my tongue ached,
make two hundred pancakes shaped like animals,
sing, and hold her as she drifted off.
But if it had already chosen sadness
or loneliness or cruelty,

any wisdom I had managed to collect
in the decades I had on her would be baby oil
on bathwater; my words, on walking out,
would twist their ankles. Still, I said my best ones,
which, if written down, would have to be revised
a hundred times, and mostly discarded.

imagining china

A foreign film in the theater of wistfulness,
it's spoken in perfect English.

Silkworms have quit making slippers for bureaucrats.
Pagodas need painting; the kitchen cat

travels the mountainside, reclining on ancestors,
not comprehending the plot. History

rests like a bear. The coup feels impossible.
We ought to fear for the sleeping rich girls,

but all will be over by nine.
We're foreigners. What we imagine

makes nothing happen; we can't even visit.
But we can't get free of the artifacts:

the book of names, outdated maps,
tailored dresses sealed in bags.

We've tried to flee the credibility,
but it sticks like infamy, so by the family

example, we're making the best of it.
Even though we have to make most of it

up – and were told fabrication
was wrong – we take up narration.

THE RE-EDUCATION OF THE INTELLECTUALS

If there had ever been a poem
in the intelligence of animals,
in uncut grass, in autumn,

it was unavailable now. Dreams
were more colorful here,
thanks to the deepness of sleep

after labor, but also more quickly
forgotten. What they happened
to have committed to memory

would have to suffice
as text. In rippling oceans
of cotton, in seas of rice,

they tried not to imagine
their daughters and sons
commanding legions

of teachers in fields of their own.
The longer the absence,
the duller the ache, but on

occasion they got a shudder
of recognition from the unlined
faces of their captors,

barely able to tower, so certain
of their rightness, they'd die
for a phrase. Soon their ignorance

would be full-grown. Could it be
reversed? How would they take
the murders and suicides, cities

on fire, reparations? If fate were
to jail them, even with books,
would they ever be able to enter?

ABC

Heard but not read—
elementary, it demanded

no explanation. Anyone
could pronounce it, even

an FOB. First in my class
to have a Hello Kitty bag,

I'd long known punctuation
that gave away nothing,

like my grandfather's card: *May this dragon
brings you, good luck and fortune.*

In garish restaurants whose menus
had the world's best typos,

waiters deciding how much ice water
to pour would ask the younger

among us, "ABC?" Only an idiot
wouldn't get it

(and we knew idiots, who screamed
Chinese, Japanese! at us and Koreans),

but decades later, mother of two,
I'm beginning to feel like a fool

for not knowing how to write it:
"American-Born Chinese"? Or might it

be "American Born, Chinese"?
Or "American, Born Chinese"?

Could it be comma- and hyphen-less?
An atrocity like "Toys 'R' Us"?

Anyway, I may now prefer hot tea.
Everything's stiff, winter to spring,

and a thousand things I uttered
in youth have been returned to sender,

for instance, "I'm not really Southern,"
then, "It's a Southern thing, you wouldn't

understand," and yesterday, "I was born
in Georgia Baptist; *that's* where I'm from."

Eventually a gift for grammar
turned me professor,

and for a while being Asian
came into fashion,

but often the antecedent
still escapes me. My grandparents'

English having gone into
the ground, I resist giving in to

silence, but when some kid shouts
Look at these! I think someone ought

to intervene, teach decency,
but – apologies – it won't be me,

as I can't dig up a single word
that would begin to be understood.

in THe counTry

I've forgotten the past again.
How many times will it happen?

You're my link to the people.
I never dreamed of being local

but never meant to be eclipsed.
Now I'm downright wifely, as if

you were the human and I the dog,
fully possessed of teeth, a strong

body, intelligence, but inexplicably
appended, looking up. Don't get me

wrong – people are *nice,* there'd be
no harm to me alone, but I wouldn't be

here alone. I'd be in the city, a book,
the university, lost in what looks

like nothing – a fraudulent character,
a disembodied voice – and never

try the church ladies' ham-and-bean soup.
Yes, I'd miss out, not just on food

but on benevolence, the care with which
they ladle it into the cup, and this

is why we've journeyed here, practically
in love – but you know what *practically*

means, reverse of *ideally*. Real love
is a novel: the author's going to have

to wrap it up. I wish *practically*
were the point. I do. I wish it bodily.

AFTERWARDS

he reveals what couldn't be said pre-kiss:
how it almost hurt
when you appeared in the burgundy dress,

how fiercely he'd experienced your split
second of hesitation by phone,
how many times he'd awakened with

the concept of you, and how he'd begun
to set the hundred tiny goals that would
make you his. You like it, being taken

back in time, blessed by sureness,
retroactively admired: it makes you feel
famous. But something in you wishes

he'd quit the piecemeal baring of ulterior
motives, the revision of memory
that makes it forever both-of-yours,

even as you crave the knowledge. And yet
you don't stop him. It's too good,
going backstage, learning how the rabbit

got into the hat. It's like literary criticism:
you can't help it, you were born
curious. And you're going to love him,

confession will beget confession,
and then you'll be exchanging
everything forbidden in the fine oblivion

that is lying together at night. It's hopeless—
understanding is irresistible,
so you let him rewrite everything, even as

you mourn the uncertainties: what his words
were really saying, what you were in his
imagination, why, and what he was in yours.

III

summer

Everyone knows about summer:
it finally fails to deliver
the goods. It singes your skin,
rains on your reading list,
insidiously lets you sleep in.
It sneakily sends up blossoms
so gorgeous and fleet-footed
you hardly notice them
going to seed. A beautiful woman
or beautiful man, it tears off
your clothing, leaves you forlorn.
Since it's all that December is not,
it's all you desire, all you regret
having let back in. In September
you cross your heart, murmur *Never
again*. And each spring you forget
how you wept, the wasted weeks
and unreturned calls. Around slinks
June, sweetly inquiring, What books
have you written me? Where
have you been? Please oh please
come along… Your compass,
memory, gut cry *No*, but you act
like you've only been born.
One bright look from the merciless
hottest of seasons, and you go.

georgia

1983. It hasn't fallen into the well
of memory yet. July, August: I still
think it's home. At Stone Mountain
the young move in packs. Everyone
at the laser show seems certain
of what they want, that they can
find it locally. I'm in high school,
no one strikes me as regional,
and I lack the range to imagine
we'll mock the way we lived, ringing
the mountain like pilgrims as it went
from green to red, to the shrill laments
of pop stars who'd finally date us.

The newest era always shines brightest,
though some predict we'll later regret
velour and emulating Farrah Fawcett.
And I've no clue how crazily I'll love
the cold Northeast, how cruelly leave
my sweetest but not last Southern boy
in the dust of my hope, or how perfectly
unoriginal that is, as all the seekers here
will do the same, or nearly: turn traitor
on our prior selves as if no longer Southern
despite the glow by which we loved them.

THE OUTER CAPE

Dozens of us hung on there, trying to love
the moment, trying not to need belongings.
Daily, the light poured in, requesting something,

and thinking we'd know better what to make
without the confusion of money, we pledged
not to need it, even as we hit the lower edge

of no longer being young. Renunciation
began to look less voluntary; onerous
questions cropped up in the gorgeous

middle of the dunes: What if this *is* the future?
What if that crying seagull isn't the ghost
of anyone, but a bird, simply using its voice?

Through snowstorms and power failures
we were bound to each other by collective
emigration, until we began to get picked off,

one by one, by fame or love or the system,
leaving the rest to wrestle with our senses
of conviction. As the ice along Route 6

turned back to water, the hordes returned
to take our lonesome beaches; we fumed
as we made their coffee, as if they'd ruined

everything, stomped on our purpose,
as if we'd hit the damaged area of a map
we were trying, even as we traveled, to unfold.

Harvard

As if boys and girls were the same,
we wandered into each other's rooms
without shoes, breakfasted together,

marched through the Cambridge snow
in packs, obscuring individual hopes.
At last, to be no one, not brainy,

not ethnic! We stayed up all night
debating right and wrong; sometimes
we called ourselves women

and men, although it still felt odd.
Houses full of children lingered as backdrop,
paused like videotape, as we browsed

the course catalog, jammed with glory,
nearly as fat as *The Joy of Cooking*.
But sometimes Cambridge felt suspiciously

like the malls we thought we'd never roam
the old way again, sixteen and lonesome
for a purpose. Nobel professor, flirt skirt,

Coop or Gap, what difference if you were only
browsing? We put on caps and gowns
as tanks rolled through Tiananmen Square;

we found the loves we would have chosen
Freshman Week if we'd been paying attention.
Though we despised the idea that college

wasn't real — wasn't it part of life, to think? —
we found ourselves that June, as in a dream,
pressed by a crowd to the front of a line

to check out of a vast department store,
giving over all our cash for a hoard
of unknown garments, most of which barely fit.

THe yoga class

Oblivious to having just walked in
on Yoga for the HIV-Positive,
we lay our bodies down among the men,
the sun the only light. We've lived

the same twenty-three years and come
to the city for what we're both sure
is the beginning. The teacher's solemn
greeting is shadowed in mercy;

we've never been the only women
in a yoga class, but this is New York.
Anything can happen. The men
are unusually beautiful, the work

too easy. Their thin limbs rise then fall
to rest in *savasana*, corpse pose,
flawlessly beside us as we struggle
with racing minds and the odd sense

of being the strongest. The others
seem to see and not see us. Late
in the hour, we discover our error.
The teacher says *Please don't make*

the mistake again. We exit with apologies,
invaders from the land of health,
emerging into the shimmering hallway
as if from underground, and steal forth

into our futures.
                    Now my friend's gone,
too, and I live in the country with children,
whose questions go without transition
from *Is Grandma's mama dead?* to *When*

will the newt grow its tail back? which I try
to answer well if not correctly, from
every angle they invent, despite
my ignorance of death and regeneration,

because it's become my job to give
what it takes, even when forced
to go the long way, over and over, as if
we had all the time in the world.

THE STARVING-ARTIST YEARS

No one knew they would end in disaster.
Because imagination was the only future,

So was the present. The permanent address
Brought about the death kiss, minus the kiss.

Late Twenties

I spent them in cloistered domesticity,
forgetting the continents I meant to visit.
Trading unease for the equanimity
of years spent in cloistered domesticity,
I had peaceful, wifely anonymity:
clean sheets, daffodils, dinner in minutes.
Thus they went, in cloistered domesticity.
I've forgotten what continents I meant to visit.

THE BRAIN GODDESS AND THE SEX GODDESS MEET AT MACY'S

twenty years post-graduation, having never
been in touch. Colliding with hangers
in children's or men's, both recall the era

of government by clothes and body,
then laugh like friends who've suddenly
forgotten the rift. Each has been ruined

and reborn, each found her place;
neither remembers having tried to disgrace
the other, yet both recall being dogged

by otherly doubt. Up from the canyon of loss
rise their common dead – the boy who crashed
the sedan, the girl with cancer, grandparents,

parents, now half a dozen teachers –
and here among the shirts they're almost sisters,
bound not by blood but by shared

finitude. Always, it began with the body,
a chill. Then the mind began its northerly
journey, starting to storm. And later, the body

brought cold of a different order. And near
it – in it – the mind, accepting the scars,
the simmering knowledge, wept real tears.

Animal Mornings

It's been so long since anyone called me "filly,"
even in memory, I can't see myself as "chick."
"Bird" permits a few more years, even decades,
but doesn't mesh with my litter, and besides,
it's somewhat sick. "Kitten" makes me laugh too hard,

but as I age I'm increasingly prone to wake
as if clothed in feathers, fur, or hide,
unready for what man is going to shout.
Language doesn't serve me, nor do my eyes;
I'm half in the ground, even as the words imply

a fair degree of spunk. Hens cluck; vixens snap;
a shrew keeps yelling; mares throw; even a cow
makes milk and bats dark lashes. Biddy, sow, gyp,
minx – all I can say has already been said, like this,
a million times: Some days, I can be a real bitch.

sestina

First, get acquainted his words,
no touch, my grandmother
might have said, generic wisdom
in a particular voice, *no one want*
woman too easy to love.
But she never lived in English; her time

came long before Nixon and the time
in my life when any such words
would have weight. Which is OK. I loved,
sometimes preferred, to dream up the grandmother
I couldn't meet. So the day you said you wanted
me, I knew the score. Conventional wisdom

on male desire is barely even wisdom –
everyone knows it – but you'd timed
it well, I didn't love you either, and wanted
you, too. And you used the right words,
sweet ones my composite grandmother
would have approved; you didn't say *love*

but planned around my plans, spoke as if in love,
locked in the first-person plural. Wisdom
could make allowances. Grandmothers
mean to snare a man till the end of time,
and I knew from your take on the printed word
that you-till-the-end-of-time was not what I wanted,

but another thing I never wanted
was a cynical absence of love,
so I let myself savor your words,
cradled in a future tense, benevolent wisdom
nestled in platitudes, and in our brief time
of *no touch*, allowed the mental grandmother

to give you *thumb up*. The real grandmother—
who knows what she would have wanted?
Maybe she would've said, *This time*
different; for this man, first-sight love;
maybe she abhorred the limits of ancient wisdom
on female joy. So I took you at your word.

Now I'm putting words in my grandmother's
mouth again, vessels for wisdom that's wanting:
Tell bad man, I will not love you long time.

THE RIFT

It started with wanting to minimize harm:
one small injury too quickly forgiven,
then a near-cruelty, until the norm
became hurt and forgiveness.

With time it became a practical matter:
so much had been invested, as in long
math, that to catch the initial error
now would cost too much. They clung

to the anecdotal – sinking cathedrals,
leaning towers that somehow remained –
so when the rift occurred, its signals
were like a minor earthquake's, so faint

the humans didn't feel a thing. No china
rattled. But the animals sickened and hid,
neglected their food. If only hindsight
could be moved – the people would

have heard the dread in every furry chest.
Still, any vet would have told them the same:
Your beloved is dying. You would be kindest
not to fight it, but to deliver her from pain.

Takeout

When she told him, he realized he hadn't
not expected it. And while he wasn't

undone, he hadn't prepared for the largeness
of the house or the grainy white expanse

of afternoons when his only purpose
was walking the dog. It was vertiginous,

he might have told her, if she were there.
Although he hadn't been happy in years,

he'd grown used to the equilibrium,
the death of intent. Their life had become

like a board game: gratuitous, provisional,
something to do. Alone in the kitchen,

eating General Tso's chicken with a plastic
fork, he tried to identify the emphatic

event he'd expected to catapult them
into life. Grandchildren, locusts, a million

bucks? For ages he'd lain indifferently
beside her, having long ago stopped listening

to her friendly and not-so-friendly suggestions,
and waited for the future to come. Wasn't

that what they'd agreed on, to endure together
all that happened from then to whenever

death did them part? Almost having eaten
a red chili, he spat it out. It lay defeated

on his plate like a dead person in a shower
of rice. That's when he understood the how

and why. He'd been waiting for someone
or something to strike down one of them

and free the other from the contract; he'd
never had a preference for which, and had

finally outwaited her. She was the villain,
but it was both of their deliverance.

He stood up suddenly, almost tripping
on the dog. He threw the dog a dumpling

and grabbed the leash and keys, without
even thinking. It was time to go out.

witness

How is it so many think they know
who left whom and why, who owed
whom how much and didn't pay,
who saw what with jaundiced eye,
whose indulgence sank the family ship,
who sulked bitterly, who threw fits,
who observed the vows in letter
but not in spirit, who got clobbered
when discussions deadlocked,
what form the abuse took,

obvious (hitting) or insidious (hinting),
who held from the beginning
alternate loyalties that in retrospect
should have been obvious, who left
the dirty work to the other, who lacked
the self-respect to refuse it; who sat
up in bed one morning and thought
This is not working and without
even knowing it set the split in motion?
Even if the court of public opinion

is airily conceptual, it has its podium,
its jury box of clouds, its white stone
steps giving foothold to those
who hold their versions close
enough to believe while the two
at the center try to stay unmoved
as the two on top of the cake, till the day
the kids are old enough to corroborate
their memories (they were only children)
of what they think must have happened.

THE MUSE AS MIDDLE-AGED MAN

I'd tell him he's been in my dreams,
but he knows when I'm making things up.
It poisons everything, from coffee to kisses.

I'd lure him with a four-course meal,
but he hates it when I cook all day.
Nice waste of your talent, he hisses.

Long ago, we stopped having arguments.
He has no logic, and it drove me batty,
academically mapping my ideas.

For a while I dressed in tailored suits
but felt misrepresented. He called them
corporate, even worse than pajamas.

(Pajamas might as well have been nothing.
We'd fuck; I'd sleep; he'd go in search
of someone who took him seriously.)

I used to win his aggravated longing
by showing up late or not at all,
but that lost its charm pretty quickly.

Nor was it my nature. I'm nine parts
scrupulous, can barely stand to stand
a man up, would gladly find my rapture

in organization instead of an art,
but not while he's offering the prospect,
again and again and again, of capture.

Renunciation

If the windows were shady enough,
if you could forget the language,

if it were possible to live untouched
by weather, even on the sunniest

of holidays, if you could conceive
of your wishes, then believe

you never really wanted them
(and live the not-wanting), then

you might be able to do it. Although
you know not to bother, knowing

has never been sufficient, so you try
to go it alone like the bravest of climbers,

like a first-time schoolteacher,
like the terrified teenagers

who keep the secret until there's no more
holding back nature, and over and over

find yourself back where you started,
wanting the thing you so cleverly put

behind you, stunned as the day
you were born, when you wailed

at the injustice, flailing, chagrined,
until someone took you into her arms.

Chinese, a Found Poem
selected entries from *The New Shorter Oxford English Dictionary*, 1993

Chinese box each of a nest of boxes

Chinese compliment a pretended deference to the opinions of others, when one's mind is already made up

Chinese copy a slavish imitation

Chinese puzzle an intricate puzzle or problem

Chinese wall *fig.* an insurmountable barrier

Chinese whispers a game in which a message is distorted by being passed around in a whisper (also called *Russian scandal*)

in THe New WorLD

Claiming to despise tradition,
they live in oblivion, in the gap
between destruction and creation.
Having broken being all they have,
they're more susceptible to hatred,
bitterness; they don't know what
to do when the children wake up
singing *O say can you see* as if it
were natural, as if there were nothing
wrong with living or even having been
born here. Clinging now for clinging's
sake, the no-longer immigrants
renounce, denounce, condemn, reject
until there's nothing to embrace;
they've no choice now but to invent.
What they beget in this interim, made
in ignorance and doubt, is crueler
than anything the ancestors pressed;
the laws, made in minutes, are wayward
as a dictator's, and as comfortless.

His Father's Son

Though his face was a carbon copy, there was plenty
he hadn't inherited: the loping walk, the nerve
to tell it like it was, the indifference to what anybody
thought. Unlike his dad, he tended to go too far
in deference to others. He gave up his chair, offered
money and food, never asked for his books back.
Where his father would have left without a word,
he tended to ramble, apologize for crimes that had
nothing to do with him. His mother imagined she'd
slighted or overprotected him. He knew himself,
knew what he was entitled to, but determined he'd
missed some basic wiring, the part that in animals
asserts the right to occupy a space. Even as an infant
in arms, he'd seemed unsure he intended to be there.
Now five foot ten, he still walked into spaces as if
the seat reserved for him must be in another car
or waiting room or auditorium, where he'd have gone
if he had found the door. No fool, he knew it existed
only in his mind, but his mind was a gigantic region,
bigger than Texas or the Great Wall of China. Even if
he never got to enter, much less sit down in it,
he knew it was there, and wouldn't quit the search for it.

Exchange

No longer clear what direction is west
More not less a minority
Disinclined to pray yet not godless
As a horde of elbows under one authority

Cigarette smoke billows out of the past
The bicycle collides with the washing
Night into day, fancy into fact
Revolution still the fashion

Tell the whiz kids, the Homecoming Court
Beauties who seize their origins—
FedEx them a postcard on a horse
The title still begins with Foreign

NOBODY SAID

I would enter the city
of birth and death,
be gouged in the marketplace,
inhabit the deepest
joy and culpability,
and be unable to communicate.

Dependent as never before
just as people and words began
to fail me, I'd operate machinery
that had never been tested,
then be held liable
for the whole of the factory.

At last I'd be torn,
not limb from limb
as in mythology,
but like a sheet of paper
on which I'd started a song
they wouldn't give back to me.

Acknowledgments

The following poems originally appeared in these journals, some in slightly different form:

The Antioch Review: "On Not Writing in Cafés"
Crab Orchard Review: "In Labor"
Crazyhorse: "The Baby Years," "His Father's Son"
Eclipse: "The Muse as Middle-Aged Man," "Nobody Said"
Electronic Poetry Review: "The Re-Education of the Intellectuals"
Emprise Review: "The Women and the Girls"
Fledgling Rag: "ABC," "In the New World," "March Comes in Like a Lion,"
    "Why It Happened," "Witness"
Gargoyle: "Harvard"
Green Mountains Review: "Middle of Nowhere"
Indiana Review: "The Love Boat"
MiPoesias: "Child," "Sestina"
New Letters: "Reading"
Oxford American: "Even the Overachievers Had Barbies," "Georgia"
Poet Lore: "Animal Mornings," "The Rift"
PoetryMagazine.com: "Imagining China," "In Spite of Great Difficulty"
Prairie Schooner: "Having It All," "The Outer Cape," "Summer"
Southwest Review: "T. J. Maxx"

Most of the poems in this book would not have been written without the generous and timely support of the Central Pennsylvania Consortium/Mellon Foundation, Dickinson College, the National Endowment for the Arts, and the Virginia Center for Creative Arts, to all of which I am grateful.

For literary and real-world insight and support, I also wish to thank Jennifer Joseph, Faith Shearin, Melanie Sumner, Cleopatra Mathis, Chris Francese and Amy Luckett, Lynn Johnson, Cotten Seiler, Elizabeth Lee, Nitsa Kann, Rebecca and Justin Marquis, Sharon O'Brien, Victoria Sams, Regina Sweeney and Gerry Murphy, and Jeff Wood. Thanks as ever to my parents, Jennifer and Kendall Su, and my brother, Jonathan Su. And daily thanks to my daughters, for making everything new.

In Memoriam: Akiyu Hatano